A Love Beyond Words: My Own Way of Saying I Love You

Kyu? Hai na special?, Volume 2

Mrigendra Bharti

Published by Sellbrochure Vymish Entertainment, 2024.

While every precaution has been taken in the preparation of this book, the publisher assumes no responsibility for errors or omissions, or for damages resulting from the use of the information contained herein.

A LOVE BEYOND WORDS: MY OWN WAY OF SAYING I LOVE YOU

First edition. September 11, 2024.

Copyright © 2024 Mrigendra Bharti.

ISBN: 979-8227433091

Written by Mrigendra Bharti.

Table of Contents

For Her

To Light of my Days,

This book is a testament to you, a canvas where every word, every poem is painted with the hues of my deepest affection. As you turn these pages, know that each line is a reflection of how uniquely you inspire me. This collection of verses is not just poetry—it is my way of saying that you are unlike anyone else in my life.

In a world filled with ordinary expressions, I wanted to give you something extraordinary. I wanted to craft a tribute that is as distinctive and beautiful as you are. Each poem here is a whisper of my admiration for you, a celebration of the way you brighten my world. Your presence in my life is a rare and wonderful gift, and I wanted to capture that uniqueness in these verses.

Your smile, your laughter, and the way you light up even the dullest days are the true muses behind this book. It's a journey through my feelings, expressed in ways that I hope will make your heart flutter and your cheeks blush. You deserve nothing less than a love that is as special as you are.

So as you read through these poems, remember that they are crafted with you in mind. They are my way of showing you just how much you mean to me, and how deeply I cherish every moment we share. This book is for you, and you alone—my muse, my inspiration, my everything.

With all my love,
Mrigendra Bharti

Preface

In a world where words are often spoken with familiarity and routine, A Love Beyond Words: My Own Way of Saying I Love You seeks to transcend the ordinary. This collection of poems is not merely a compilation of verses but a deeply personal expression of affection crafted with an uncommon touch.

Each poem within these pages is inspired by a singular individual whose presence has profoundly influenced my heart and thoughts. This book serves as a testament to the unique and extraordinary nature of the person who has inspired these words. It is an attempt to convey feelings of admiration and love in a way that is both original and heartfelt.

The title itself suggests a journey beyond conventional expressions, aiming to explore the depths of emotion through a personal and creative lens. Here, "I Love You" is not just a phrase but an experience—a sentiment expressed in a manner that is as unique as the muse who inspired it.

As you turn these pages, you will find that each poem is a reflection of a distinct and cherished bond. This work is dedicated to celebrating a presence that brings light and grace into every moment, transforming ordinary days into something extraordinary.

May these verses offer a glimpse into a love that is both profound and beautifully expressed, and may they resonate with anyone who has ever experienced the magic of admiration and affection in its truest form.

Series Overview: Kyu? Hai na Special?

In a world where expressions of love often blend into the mundane, Kyu? Hai na Special? stands as a beacon of originality. This series, crafted with deep admiration and affection, explores a distinctive approach to celebrating someone truly exceptional.

The title itself poses a question that invites curiosity—why is this approach special? The answer lies in the way each book is meticulously designed to honor a singular muse, whose essence and charm transcend the ordinary. Every poem and every word within these pages are dedicated to a princess-like figure, embodying grace and elegance that inspire each verse.

As you journey through this series, you will discover that each book is not just a collection of poems but a tribute to a unique individual whose impact is both profound and unparalleled. The distinctive approach captured in these works reflects a heartfelt dedication, celebrating a presence that turns the everyday into something extraordinary.

Kyu? Hai na Special? is more than just a title—it is a declaration of the exceptional nature of the muse behind these verses and an invitation to experience love expressed in a truly remarkable way.

Acknowledgment

In the quiet moments of reflection, I find myself overwhelmed with gratitude for the inspiration behind this book. This collection of poems is dedicated to a remarkable presence, a person whose essence has infused every word and sentiment within these pages.

To the one whose grace and charm have transformed the ordinary into the extraordinary, I extend my deepest thanks. Your influence has shaped these verses and turned them into a celebration of the unique and the beautiful. It is your spirit that has guided each line, and your elegance that has inspired each thought.

Though your name remains unspoken, your impact is profoundly felt in every stanza. This book stands as a testament to the admiration and affection you have sparked. Your presence has been the muse that turned fleeting moments into lasting expressions of love.

Thank you for being a beacon of inspiration. This work is a tribute to you and a reflection of the exceptional qualities that make you truly special.

With heartfelt appreciation,
Mrigendra Bharti

About Sellbrochure IPDP

Sellbrochure Vymish Entertainment, recognized as India's largest book publishing company, has made significant strides in ensuring its extensive collection of books reaches audiences across the global market. This rapid expansion is a testament to the company's dedication to disseminating knowledge and literature far beyond national borders. Central to its success is its affiliation with InkWhirl Media Networks, a reputable entity in the media and publication industry known for its innovative and strategic approaches. Within this network, InkWhirl Publication LLC operates as a vital division, further enhancing the company's capabilities and reach in the international market.

The visionary behind this enterprise is Mrigendra Bharti, the founder of Sellbrochure Vymish Entertainment. His foresight and passion for the literary world have been instrumental in steering the company towards remarkable growth and recognition. Under his leadership, Sellbrochure Vymish Entertainment has not only expanded its catalog but also established a strong presence in both domestic and international markets. Mrigendra Bharti's commitment to excellence and innovation has been a driving force in the company's journey, ensuring that it stays ahead of industry trends and meets the evolving needs of readers worldwide.

Sellbrochure Vymish Entertainment operates under the robust support of its parental organization, Mrigendra Bharti Group InfoTech. This affiliation provides the necessary resources and strategic guidance, enabling the publishing company to undertake ambitious projects and explore new markets. Mrigendra Bharti Group InfoTech's extensive experience in technology and information services has been a valuable asset, allowing Sellbrochure Vymish Entertainment to integrate advanced digital solutions in its operations, thereby enhancing its distribution capabilities and reader engagement.

Through relentless efforts and a commitment to quality, Sellbrochure Vymish Entertainment continues to break barriers and expand the reach of Indian literature globally. The company's diverse portfolio includes a wide range of genres, catering to different age groups and interests, thereby fostering a rich and inclusive reading culture. As it continues to innovate and grow, Sellbrochure Vymish Entertainment remains dedicated to its mission of making literature accessible to all, contributing significantly to the global literary landscape.

Connect With Mrigendra,
Thank you very much for choosing this book.
You can also connect with me on Instagram,
https://www.instagram.com/i_mrigendrabharti.official
With Love,
Mrigendra Bharti

Introduction

Welcome to A Love Beyond Words: My Own Way of Saying I Love You. This collection is a heartfelt exploration of love expressed through a series of poems crafted to convey what words alone often struggle to capture. Each verse is a reflection of deep admiration and affection, penned in a style that seeks to go beyond the usual declarations of love.

The inspiration for this book comes from an extraordinary individual whose presence has profoundly influenced my life. This muse, whose impact is felt in every line and stanza, has turned everyday moments into sources of inspiration and wonder. This collection is dedicated to celebrating her unique grace and charm in a manner that is both personal and distinctive.

The poems within these pages are not mere expressions of love but are crafted to showcase the depth and originality of this affection. Each poem is a tribute to a relationship that defies the ordinary, capturing feelings in a way that is as unique as the person who inspired them.

As you read through this collection, I hope you find a sense of connection and appreciation for the creative ways in which love can be expressed. This book is an invitation to experience love through a fresh and personal lens, celebrating the extraordinary nature of someone who has redefined what it means to be special.

Thank you for joining me on this journey of expression and discovery. May these poems resonate with you and offer a new perspective on the beauty of love.

A Heartfelt Harmony

Your laughter's music to my ears,
Chasing away all doubts and fears.
Your eyes, a galaxy, vast and deep,
Where my love and dreams forever sleep.
With you, my love, life's a melody,
A symphony of joy, just you and me.
Your touch, a gentle summer breeze,
Brings comfort and eternal ease.
You're the missing piece to my soul's art,
Forever etched deep within my heart.
I'm grateful for you, every single day,
In every way, words can't convey.

Sun Kissed Love

Your smile, a sunrise, bright and new,
Illuminates my world, just for you.
With you, my love, I've found my way,
To a love that's here to stay.
Your heart, a garden, sweet and fair,
Where love and happiness always share.
You're the reason for my every breath,
My guiding star, beyond death.
I'll cherish you, come what may,
You're the sunshine in my day.

Forever and a Day

Your love, a treasure, pure and true,
A gift from heaven, sent to you.
With you, my love, I'm lost in a dream,
A perfect world, it does seem.
Your touch, a gentle summer rain,
Washing away all sorrow and pain.
I'm lucky to have you, my love,
A gift from above.
Forever and a day, I'll say,
I'm yours in every way.

Whispers of the Moonlight

In the still of night, beneath the glowing sky,
Your name, like a whisper, to the stars, I cry.
Every twinkling light is a secret I hold,
Of the love in my heart, untold and bold.
Your smile is the dawn, the first touch of sun,
And when you're near, my world is spun.
I may not say it loud, but in my gaze you'll see,
Every beat of my heart says "You belong with me."
If words could carry the depth of my soul,
"I love you" wouldn't be enough to make me whole.
Yet, here I stand, with feelings so true,
In each silent moment, I'm loving you.

Waves of My Heart

Like the ocean's tide that comes and goes,
My love for you endlessly flows.
With every ripple that touches the shore,
I love you more than ever before.
Your laugh, like the wind, dances in the air,
In every moment, I see you there.
Though I say nothing, my heart speaks clear,
"I love you" in silence, always near.
If distance grows, and clouds may part,
Remember, you're the waves in my heart.
Through every storm, and gentle breeze,
With you, my soul finds its peace.

The Silent Bloom

In the quiet bloom of a flower's grace,
I see your beauty in every space.
Each petal, soft, whispers your name,
And with every breath, it feels the same.
You may not hear the words I say,
But "I love you" lingers in every way.
With every glance, and every touch,
Know that you mean so very much.
If ever you're lost, just close your eyes,
Feel my love beneath the skies.
For in the silence, in nature's hue,
My heart will always call to you.

Whispers of the Moonlight (extended)

In the quiet night, beneath the stars so bright,
I whisper your name, under the silver light.
The moon listens close, as I softly confess,
My love for you, though I speak it less.
Your smile is the dawn, that lights up my day,
Like the first sunbeam, chasing darkness away.
I see you in dreams, and feel you in air,
Even when you're not near, I know you're there.
Every breeze that passes, carries my plea,
A silent "I love you," just waiting to be.
In your eyes, I see the world so true,
Every beat of my heart, beats just for you.
If words could hold all I wish to say,
"I love you" would bloom like flowers in May.
So, if you're ever lost in the night's soft hue,
Remember, my whispers are all for you.

Waves of My Heart (extended)

Like the waves that kiss the endless shore,
My love for you grows more and more.
In every splash, in every tide,
My feelings for you I cannot hide.
Your laugh is the breeze that sweeps the sea,
Bringing calm, bringing peace, just for me.
And though the ocean may seem wide,
I'm always right here, by your side.
When I say nothing, know this is true,
My heart softly whispers, "I love you."
Like the waves returning to the sand,
I'll always come back, holding your hand.
So when the storms may rise and roar,
Just look at the sea, and know for sure,
No matter how far the winds may blow,
My love for you will always flow.

The Silent Bloom (extended)

In the garden of life, a flower blooms rare,
Your beauty and grace are beyond compare.
With every petal, soft and bright,
You bring warmth to my darkest night.
I don't need words, I don't need sound,
In your presence, my love is found.
Like a flower turning towards the sun,
My heart is yours, you're the only one.
Each breeze that passes, carries my care,
A quiet "I love you," floating in the air.
And when you're near, time stands still,
In your smile, my soul finds its will.
So when you wonder, or doubt my heart,
Know from the start, you've had every part.
In this silent bloom, with petals so true,
Every breath I take, is a gift to you.

Stars in Your Eyes

When I look at the stars, I see your face,
In every twinkle, there's your grace.
Your eyes hold galaxies, deep and wide,
I find my world when I'm by your side.
The night is quiet, but my heart's loud,
Whispering "I love you," without a crowd.
In every blink, in every smile,
You make this life so worthwhile.
I may not always say it clear,
But in my silence, know I'm here.
Like the stars that shine through the darkest night,
You are my guide, my endless light.
So if you ever feel alone in the skies,
Just close your eyes, and realize,
I'm loving you in every way,
In the light, in the dark, every single day.

Song of the Breeze

There's a melody in the evening breeze,
A gentle whisper through the trees.
It carries my heart, soft and slow,
Telling you things I want you to know.
Your laughter is music to my soul,
With every sound, I feel more whole.
And though I may not always speak,
My love for you is never weak.
In every rustle, in every sway,
"I love you" is all I wish to say.
Like the wind that touches your face,
I long to hold you in a warm embrace.
So when you feel that soft breeze near,
Know my love is always here.
In every gust, in every song,
With you is where my heart belongs.

The Rhythm of Us

In the rhythm of life, you're my sweet tune,
Like the sun that chases away the moon.
Your voice is the song that fills my day,
In every word, I find my way.
When I see you smile, the world seems bright,
Like stars twinkling on a quiet night.
And though I may stumble, or words may miss,
Know that each moment, I cherish this bliss.
"I love you" echoes in every beat,
In your presence, I feel complete.
Though life may dance us to and fro,
You're the only rhythm I ever want to know.
So if you're ever lost in life's dance,
Take my hand, give us a chance.
In every step, in every move,
My heart will always follow your groove.

Heartbeats of the Rain

When the sky turns gray and rain starts to fall,
I feel my love in each drop's call.
Every beat of the rain against the ground,
Whispers "I love you" in a quiet sound.
Your touch is the warmth in the coldest breeze,
And when you're near, the world feels at ease.
Like raindrops dancing on windows clear,
You're the melody my heart holds dear.
I don't need the sun to brighten my day,
Your smile alone takes the clouds away.
Each step you take is poetry in motion,
And my heart, like the sea, is full of devotion.
So when it rains, and you feel the chill,
Know my love for you is standing still.
In every storm, in every refrain,
My heart will always beat with the rain.

Echoes in the Wind

As the wind moves through the trees,
It carries my heart across the seas.
Each gust whispers words you may not hear,
But trust me, my love is always near.
Your eyes are like the sky so vast,
In them, I find my future and past.
The world fades away when you're close by,
You are the reason I look to the sky.
Every breath of wind, every gentle sigh,
Is my silent "I love you," drifting high.
And when the wind calls your name so sweet,
Know it's my heart, forever on repeat.
So when you stand in the breeze alone,
Feel my love in every tone.
No matter the distance, no matter the place,
The wind will always carry my embrace.

Underneath the Willow Tree

Beneath the shade of a willow tree,
Is where my heart longs for you to be.
The branches sway, like my thoughts of you,
Whispering love in everything they do.
Your laughter echoes in the summer air,
A sound so sweet, so soft, so rare.
I sit and wonder how to say,
"I love you" in a better way.
But sometimes words aren't meant to be,
Like the silence under that willow tree.
So I'll let the wind and leaves above,
Speak for me, of endless love.
And if you ever doubt what's true,
Remember the tree that shaded you.
In every leaf that falls so slow,
Is a quiet "I love you" that you already know.

Golden Hours with You

In the golden hour, as the sun dips low,
I find your light, in its gentle glow.
Your eyes, like the sun, warm my soul,
With you beside me, I feel whole.
The sky turns pink, the air turns sweet,
And my heart races with every heartbeat.
Though I may stumble on what to say,
My love for you never fades away.
Every sunset reminds me of you,
With shades of love in every hue.
And as the day turns into night,
Your presence keeps my world alight.
So when you see that golden sky,
Know my heart is never shy.
In every color, in every hue,
I'm silently saying, "I love you."

Sunrise in Your Smile

Each morning, when the sun does rise,
I find your smile within the skies.
The warmth it brings, so soft and true,
Feels like the world is made for you.
Your laughter is the songbirds' tune,
Brightening my day before it's noon.
And though I may not say it clear,
My heart whispers, "I love you," dear.
Every sunrise, with its golden light,
Reminds me of you, pure and bright.
In your eyes, I see the day begin,
A journey of love that will never dim.
So when you wake and see the sun,
Know my heart is forever won.
With each new dawn, my love renews,
In every sunrise, I find you.

The Language of the Stars

Underneath the blanket of a starlit sky,
I silently watch as the night floats by.
Each star is a word, written in the dark,
Speaking of love with a glowing spark.
Your eyes reflect those stars so clear,
And in their light, I disappear.
I wish I could tell you all I feel,
But some things only stars reveal.
They say "I love you" without a sound,
In the heavens where no bounds are found.
And so, I'll wait in the silent night,
For you to see what feels so right.
In every twinkle, in every gleam,
You are the dream I love to dream.
So when the stars fill up your sky,
Remember, my love never says goodbye.

Dewdrops of Affection

In the early morning, soft and still,
Dewdrops gather on the windowsill.
Like them, my love is quiet and true,
A reflection of all I feel for you.
Your voice, like a breeze in the gentle dawn,
Is the melody my heart lingers on.
And though I may not always speak,
My love for you is never weak.
Each dewdrop tells a secret tale,
Of love that never fears to fail.
In every shimmer, in every glow,
"I love you" more than you'll ever know.
So when you wake and see the dew,
Know that my heart belongs to you.
In every drop, in the morning light,
My love will shine, pure and bright.

A Symphony of Quiet

In the silence of a soft spring day,
There are words I long to say.
But sometimes silence speaks so loud,
More than I could in any crowd.
Your presence is my favorite song,
A melody that carries me along.
And though the world may never know,
My love for you continues to grow.
Like music without a single note,
My feelings for you quietly float.
They fill the air with gentle sound,
A love so pure, forever bound.
So when you hear the quiet hum,
Know my love will always come.
In silence, in song, in all that's true,
Every note is my "I love you."

Beneath the Starlit Silence

In the quiet of the starlit night,
I think of you, my guiding light.
Your smile, a moon that shines so bright,
Filling my heart with endless delight.
The stars above seem to align,
Whispering softly, "You are mine."
Though words may falter, shy and few,
Know in my silence, I love you.
Each twinkling star, each beam of glow,
Carries a message you may not know.
In the vastness of the midnight sky,
My love for you will never die.
So when you gaze up at the stars tonight,
Feel my love in the soft moonlight.
In every twinkle, in every hue,
My heart beats only for you.

The Fireflies' Glow

Like fireflies dancing in the dusk,
My love for you feels light and just.
It flickers softly, pure and true,
In every glance, it grows for you.
Your laughter is like the summer breeze,
Carrying joy with perfect ease.
In every moment, silent or loud,
You make me feel both free and proud.
Though I don't say it every day,
My heart's with you in every way.
Like fireflies glowing in the night,
You are my warmth, my endless light.
So when the evening comes to play,
And fireflies guide you on your way,
Remember, my love glows just as bright,
In every flicker, in every light.

The Color of My Heart

If love could be painted, it'd wear your hue,
A vibrant blend of all that's true.
Your smile, like sunlight, warms my soul,
Turning the ordinary into something whole.
Each color, each shade, tells our story,
Of quiet love and hidden glory.
In every brushstroke, soft and light,
You fill my world with endless bright.
Though I don't speak it every time,
In every color, my love does shine.
In red, in gold, in softest blue,
Every hue whispers, "I love you."
So if you ever doubt the art we've made,
Look at the colors that will never fade.
In every stroke, in every part,
You hold the palette of my heart.

Raindrops and Roses

Like raindrops on a quiet spring day,
My love for you finds a tender way.
It falls gently, without a sound,
Yet in each drop, my heart is found.
Your presence is a blooming rose,
In its beauty, my affection grows.
With every petal, soft and bright,
You turn my world into pure light.
Though I may not always speak aloud,
My love for you is clear and proud.
In raindrops, in roses, in the air so sweet,
My heart races with every beat.
So when the rain falls from the skies,
Know that my love never hides.
In every petal, in every drop,
For you, my heart will never stop.

Sunsets and Silhouettes

As the sun dips low, casting its gold,
Your beauty is a sight I can't withhold.
In the silhouettes, soft and deep,
I find the love I wish to keep.
Your laugh is the last light of the day,
Bringing warmth as night takes sway.
And though I may not always say,
"I love you" in every possible way,
In every sunset, in every hue,
My heart belongs, only to you.
The night may fall, the day may end,
But my love for you will never bend.
So when you see the sky turn bright,
In every orange and pink twilight,
Remember this love, strong and true,
Is painted in every sunset for you.

Whispers in the Breeze

The breeze carries whispers soft and true,
Every gust is a message of "I love you."
Your voice is the melody it seeks,
Brushing past my soul when it speaks.
Each gentle wind that touches my face,
Feels like your arms in a warm embrace.
Though distance keeps us apart at times,
The wind sings your name in lovely rhymes.
I don't need words when you're in the air,
My love for you is always there.
In the quiet, in the gentle sway,
I fall for you more every day.
So when the breeze caresses your cheek,
Know it's my love, subtle yet deep.
In every gust, in every sigh,
I love you more than words can try.

Ocean's Secret Song

By the shore, where waves gently kiss,
I dream of you in every bliss.
The ocean hums a soft refrain,
Telling stories of love again and again.
Your eyes are like the deep blue sea,
Full of wonders, pulling me.
In every ripple, in every tide,
I find my heart by your side.
Even when waves seem far and wide,
My love for you won't ever hide.
Like the ocean, vast and true,
My heart flows endlessly to you.
So when you hear the ocean's tune,
In the light of the softest moon,
Know my love is as deep and wide,
As the endless ocean by your side.

Petals in the Wind

Like petals floating on a breeze,
My love for you is light and free.
It drifts and sways with every turn,
A fire in my heart that will forever burn.
Your smile is like the blooming rose,
In your beauty, my whole world glows.
And even when the petals fall,
My love for you stands strong and tall.
In every flower that blooms anew,
I see a piece of me and you.
No matter where the winds may go,
Our love is something I'll always show.
So when you see those petals fly,
Know it's my heart that will never die.
In every petal, soft and pure,
My love for you will always endure.

The Light in My Night

In the dark when the world is still,
It's your light that my heart does fill.
Like a star that shines so bright,
You are the reason I chase the night.
Your eyes, like stars, guide my way,
Even when skies are dull and gray.
In your glow, I find my peace,
A love that will never cease.
Though the night may bring its fears,
Your love wipes away my tears.
With every twinkle, with every gleam,
You are my brightest, sweetest dream.
So when the night seems dark and long,
Know my heart beats with your song.
In every star that lights the sky,
My love for you will never die.

Through the Seasons of Us

In spring, when flowers start to bloom,
I find your love in every room.
Your laughter is the morning dew,
Fresh, sweet, and always new.
In summer's warmth, your heart is bright,
Like sunshine breaking through the night.
With every ray, with every beam,
You fill my world with endless dream.
In autumn's breeze, when leaves turn gold,
Your love is a story yet untold.
Though colors fade and seasons end,
Our love will always transcend.
And in winter's cold and frosty air,
Your warmth is something none compare.
Through every season, year by year,
I love you more, my dearest dear.

Moonlight and Memories

Under the soft moon's silver glow,
There are secrets only you should know.
Like moonlight dancing on the sea,
Your love means everything to me.
Every memory we've ever made,
Shines brighter than a shooting cascade.
Even in silence, even in dreams,
Your love is more than what it seems.
In every star, in every light,
You are my constant, my shining knight.
Though nights may change, though time will pass,
My love for you will always last.
So when you look up at the moon,
And feel its gentle, quiet tune,
Remember that with every gleam,
You are the one I love to dream.

Heartbeat in the Silence

In the quiet moments when all is still,
It's your heartbeat that I feel.
A rhythm soft, a song so sweet,
With every pulse, my love's complete.
I may not say it every time,
But in your presence, I find my rhyme.
Your laughter is the music I need,
Your smile is my heart's true creed.
Even in silence, even when apart,
You are the beat within my heart.
Like a soft drum beneath the sky,
My love for you will never die.
So when you feel the world go quiet,
Know that my love is forever private.
In every beat, in every breath,
My love for you defies even death.

The Secret in the Rain

When the rain begins to fall,
I find my love in every drop, so small.
Each one carries a tale untold,
Of a love that never grows cold.
Your eyes reflect the stormy skies,
Yet in your smile, my sunshine lies.
And though the rain may hide my face,
In every drop, I find your grace.
I love you like the rain loves the earth,
Refreshing, pure, and full of worth.
No thunder, no storm, can take away,
The love I feel for you each day.
So when the rain taps on your windowpane,
Let it remind you of my love's refrain.
In every shower, in every stream,
You are the essence of my sweetest dream.

Echoes of the Forest

In the forest, deep and wide,
It's you I feel, right by my side.
Your love is the whisper in the trees,
A calming wind, a gentle breeze.
The leaves that fall, the streams that flow,
They speak of love only we know.
In every rustle, in every sound,
I find the peace that you surround.
Your touch is soft like moss and earth,
Your heart, the place I find my worth.
Though words may not always suffice,
Your love feels like paradise.
So when you walk beneath the trees,
Know that my love follows with ease.
In every echo, in every song,
My heart for you beats loud and strong.

The Glow of Your Soul

When the world turns dark and gray,
It's your glow that lights my way.
A warmth so deep, a shine so bright,
You are the lantern in my night.
Your kindness, like a gentle flame,
Burns so quietly, without shame.
And in that glow, I feel complete,
Your love, my heart's steady beat.
No storm, no shadow can hide your light,
You guide me through the darkest night.
Even when clouds block the view,
I'll always find my way to you.
So when you feel the darkness grow,
Remember, you're my constant glow.
In every flicker, in every gleam,
You are my everlasting dream.

Footprints on the Sand

On the shores where waves gently play,
I see our footprints in the sand, each day.
Side by side, we walk so free,
Your love is the ocean's melody.
The sand may shift, the tide may rise,
But your love stays constant, never disguised.
In every footprint, deep and true,
I find my heart belongs to you.
Even when the waves wash away,
Our love remains, come what may.
For in the sand, in the sea,
You are the one who completes me.
So when you feel the ocean's tide,
Know I'll always be by your side.
In every wave, in every land,
You'll find my heart in the sand.

A Garden of Forever

In the garden where flowers bloom,
I find your love in every room.
Each petal soft, each leaf so bright,
Reminds me of your gentle light.
Your heart is the soil where love grows tall,
A place where I find it all.
With every blossom, with every seed,
You are the only one I need.
The garden may change with every season,
But my love for you needs no reason.
In the rain, in the sun, in every weather,
Our hearts will bloom together forever.
So when you walk through the flowers' scent,
Know my love is forever meant.
In every bloom, in every tree,
You are my garden, endlessly.

The Dawn of Us

When the night gives way to dawn,
I feel your love as the day comes on.
Like the first light breaking the sky,
You are the reason my soul can fly.
Each sunrise brings a brand new start,
A reminder of you in my heart.
With every ray, with every glow,
I love you more than you'll ever know.
Though clouds may hide the morning sun,
My love for you is never done.
In every dawn, in every hue,
My heart belongs forever to you.
So when you wake and see the light,
Know my love will always be bright.
In every sunrise, in every day,
You are the light that leads my way.

Sunset Promises

As the sun sinks low in the sky,
I find my heart drifting nearby.
The colors blend in hues so fine,
Just like your love, so pure, divine.
In every streak of orange and gold,
Your love is the warmth I want to hold.
Even as the day turns to night,
Your smile remains my guiding light.
The sunset promises hope anew,
And whispers softly, "I love you."
Though the day may fade away,
My love for you is here to stay.
So when you see the sun descend,
Remember, my love will never end.
In every sunset, in every glow,
My heart beats for you, just so.

The Rhythm of Rain

When raindrops fall on window glass,
It's your name they softly pass.
Each drop a note in a song so sweet,
Echoing the rhythm of our heartbeat.
In every puddle, in every splash,
Your love feels like a gentle crash.
A soothing sound that fills the air,
Reminding me you're always there.
The rain may come, the storm may rise,
But in your eyes, my sunshine lies.
Even in the darkest shower,
Your love is my shelter, my power.
So when the rain begins to play,
Know I love you more each day.
In every drop, in every stream,
You are my life's most precious dream.

The Path We Walk

On the road where shadows fall,
Your love guides me through it all.
With every step, with every pace,
I find my home in your embrace.
Though the path may twist and turn,
It's your love for which I yearn.
No matter where the journey leads,
You're the one my heart needs.
Together we walk, side by side,
In your love, I take such pride.
Through every valley, over every hill,
With you, my heart is always still.
So when the road seems long and far,
Know my love is where you are.
In every step, in every mile,
You are the reason I always smile.

The Magic of Your Laugh

Your laughter is a summer breeze,
A sound that puts my soul at ease.
Each note like music in the air,
It makes me fall deeper in love, I swear.
When you laugh, the world feels light,
Everything wrong suddenly feels right.
In your joy, I find my peace,
A love that will never cease.
Even in moments dark and gray,
Your laughter shines, lighting the way.
Like a melody that never ends,
You are my heart's closest friend.
So when you laugh, remember this,
Each sound feels like the sweetest kiss.
In every giggle, in every smile,
You make my world more worthwhile.

A Flame That Never Fades

Your love is like a steady flame,
Burning bright, always the same.
In your warmth, I find my light,
Guiding me through the darkest night.
Even when the world feels cold,
Your love is the fire I want to hold.
It never flickers, it never fades,
In its glow, I feel unafraid.
Through every storm, through every fight,
Your love remains my constant light.
A flame that burns deep in my chest,
With you, I know I'm truly blessed.
So when you feel the world go dim,
Remember, my love will never trim.
In every flicker, in every glow,
You are the fire that makes me whole.

Stars Between Us

In the quiet of the night,
When stars above are shining bright,
I think of you, my love so true,
And wish upon the sky for you.
Each star is like a piece of us,
A symbol of a love so wondrous.
Though the distance may stretch wide,
You are always by my side.
Even if the stars burn out,
My love for you leaves no doubt.
In every twinkle, in every gleam,
You are my forever dream.
So when you gaze upon the stars,
Know no matter how far we are,
In every shimmer, in every light,
You are my love, my guiding sight.

Your Voice, My Home

Your voice is like a melody,
It brings my heart such harmony.
Each word you say, each gentle tone,
Makes me feel like I'm never alone.
In the quiet moments of the day,
It's your voice that lights the way.
Like a song that calms the sea,
You bring such peace inside of me.
Even when you're far from sight,
Your voice makes everything feel right.
A sound so soft, a sound so true,
I find my home inside of you.
So when you speak, just know this fact,
It's your voice that brings me back.
In every note, in every sound,
My love for you will always surround.

Whispers in the Breeze

When the soft breeze begins to blow,
It carries the love I want you to know.
In every whisper, in every sigh,
My heart calls out, you're my sky.
The wind may roam, the leaves may sway,
But my love for you will never stray.
Like a breeze that's gentle, pure, and true,
I'm forever drawn towards you.
Even if storms may cross our path,
I'll find you through the aftermath.
For in the breeze, I hear your name,
A love so strong, it's always the same.
So when the wind brushes your cheek,
Know it's my love, calm yet unique.
In every gust, in every breeze,
You're the one who gives me peace.

Dancing in Moonlight

When the moon begins to rise,
I see your love in the starry skies.
A dance so slow, so pure, so bright,
You're the moon guiding my night.
In every shimmer, in every glow,
I see the love you softly show.
Your eyes, like stars, light up the way,
Turning my night into day.
Though the moon may fade at dawn,
My love for you will carry on.
For in the dark or in the light,
You're the reason I'm alright.
So when the moon beams down on you,
Know my love is forever true.
In every phase, in every sight,
I'm dancing in your moonlit light.

The Sound of Your Smile

Your smile is like a melody,
It plays a song deep inside me.
Each curve of your lips, so bright and kind,
Lifts the weight from my weary mind.
In your smile, I find my peace,
A love that will never cease.
Even when words are left unsaid,
Your smile speaks what's in your head.
It's the sound of joy, pure and sweet,
A song that makes my heart skip a beat.
Through every day, through every while,
I live to see your gentle smile.
So when you smile, just know this truth,
It's the sound of love, pure as youth.
In every grin, in every beam,
You're the light within my dream.

# Through Every Storm

When the storm clouds gather and roar,
I find your love more than before.
In every thunder, in every rain,
You wash away all my pain.
Though the skies may darken, fierce and wild,
Your love remains, soft and mild.
Like a shelter in the fiercest gale,
With you, I know I'll never fail.
Even when lightning strikes the ground,
Your love's the calm I've always found.
In every storm, in every fight,
You're my beacon, shining bright.
So when the rain begins to fall,
Know my love will conquer all.
In every storm, in every tear,
You're the love I hold most dear.

The Echo of Your Heartbeat

In the quiet of the night,
Your heartbeat echoes soft and light.
A rhythm that I feel so near,
It's the sound that I hold dear.
Each beat, a whisper, tender and true,
A reminder of my love for you.
When the world is still and calm,
Your heartbeat is my soothing balm.
Even when distance keeps us apart,
Your rhythm guides my restless heart.
In every pulse, in every sound,
My love for you is truly found.
So when you listen to your heart's soft beat,
Know it's my love that makes it complete.
In every echo, in every sigh,
You are my forever, my reason why.

The Light You Bring

When the day turns into night,
Your love becomes my guiding light.
A beacon shining, pure and bright,
Leading me through every plight.
In the darkness, in the cold,
Your warmth is worth more than gold.
With every star that lights the sky,
It's your love that catches my eye.
Even when shadows cross my way,
Your love is my bright array.
In every twilight, in every beam,
You are my star, my cherished dream.
So when you see the stars above,
Know you are the light I love.
In every glimmer, in every ray,
You guide my heart every day.

Your Presence, My Peace

In your presence, I find my peace,
A quiet calm that will never cease.
When the world feels loud and fast,
You are the calm that makes it last.
With you, the noise fades away,
And the troubles of life seem to sway.
Your touch, your voice, your gentle grace,
Brings a soothing smile to my face.
Even when life feels rough and tough,
Your presence makes the journey enough.
In every moment, in every day,
You are my peace in every way.
So when you're near, just know this true,
My heart finds solace only in you.
In every sigh, in every calm,
You are my ever-present balm.

The Space Between Us

In the space that lies between,
It's your love that I have seen.
Though miles may stretch and time may bend,
You are the constant, my dear friend.
No distance can erase the bond,
Or make my heart any less fond.
In every breath, in every beat,
Your love is what makes me complete.
Even when we're far apart,
You're the one who fills my heart.
In every space, in every void,
You are the love I have enjoyed.
So when we're apart, remember this,
My love for you is endless bliss.
In every moment, near or far,
You are my guiding star.

In the Silence of the Night

In the silence of the night so deep,
It's your love that I long to keep.
When stars are out and shadows play,
You are the light that guides my way.
In every quiet, in every hush,
Your love creates a gentle rush.
A whisper soft, a touch so kind,
You're the peace I always find.
Even when the night is long and cold,
Your warmth is a love I hold.
In every dream, in every thought,
You're the love I always sought.
So when the night is calm and still,
Know my love for you will fill.
In every silence, in every star,
You are my love, no matter how far.

The Magic of Your Touch

Your touch is like a magic spell,
A feeling I know so well.
With every brush, with every caress,
You bring a calm, a soft finesse.
In your touch, I find my peace,
A love that will never cease.
Even when words fail to say,
Your touch lights up my day.
Though the world may sometimes tire,
Your touch is my heart's desire.
In every moment, in every feel,
Your touch makes my love real.
So when you reach out, just know this,
Your touch is my eternal bliss.
In every caress, in every kiss,
You are my heart's truest wish.

The Journey of Us

On the journey that we share,
You are the love that's always there.
Through every step, through every mile,
You make my life so worthwhile.
Though paths may wind and roads may bend,
Your love is where my heart will send.
In every turn, in every pace,
You are my steady, loving grace.
Even when the road is rough and long,
Your love is my guiding song.
In every journey, in every stride,
You are the joy that's by my side.
So when the road is dark and deep,
Know my love for you will keep.
In every step, in every lane,
You are my love, through joy and pain.

The Light in Your Eyes

In the depths of your lovely eyes,
I see a world where my heart flies.
A spark that dances, bright and clear,
Bringing warmth to all I hold dear.
Each glance, a promise of love so true,
A beacon guiding me back to you.
In the twinkle, in the shine,
I find a love that's purely mine.
Even in moments dark and cold,
Your eyes are the light I long to hold.
In every gaze, in every spark,
You are my guiding, shining mark.
So when you look my way, just know,
Your eyes are where my feelings grow.
In every glance, in every stare,
You are the light beyond compare.

The Song of Your Heart

Your heart sings a melody so sweet,
A rhythm that makes my life complete.
Each beat a note in a love song true,
A symphony that's always new.
In every pulse, in every sound,
A love so deep, so profound.
Even when words can't convey,
Your heart's song guides my way.
Though the world may sometimes drown,
Your melody lifts me up from down.
In every chord, in every beat,
You make my life feel so complete.
So when you listen to your heart's song,
Know it's where my love belongs.
In every tune, in every sound,
You are the love I've truly found.

In Your Warm Embrace

In your warm and gentle embrace,
I find a peaceful, tender place.
A haven where my heart can rest,
A love that's simply the best.
Each hug, a promise, soft and tight,
Wrapping me in pure delight.
Even when the world feels cold,
Your embrace is worth more than gold.
In every touch, in every hold,
You are the love that makes me bold.
So when you hold me close, my dear,
Know my love is always near.
In every embrace, in every squeeze,
You are my heart's deepest peace.

The Fire in Your Kiss

Your kiss is a fire that warms my soul,
A flame that makes me feel whole.
With every touch, with every press,
You ignite a passion that I confess.
In each kiss, I find a spark,
A love that's bright, even in the dark.
Though the world may sometimes tire,
Your kiss rekindles my heart's fire.
Even when life seems cold and gray,
Your kiss brings warmth to my day.
In every touch, in every kiss,
You are my love, my sweetest bliss.
So when you kiss me, just know this,
You're the flame I can't resist.
In every press, in every trace,
You are the warmth I embrace.

The Path of Our Love

On the path where we both tread,
You are the light that guides ahead.
Through every twist, through every turn,
It's your love that makes me yearn.
In each step, in every mile,
You make the journey so worthwhile.
Even when the road is tough and long,
You are my constant, loving song.
Though the path may twist and wind,
Your love is the peace I find.
In every journey, in every stride,
You are the joy that walks beside.
So as we travel, side by side,
Know my love is your guide.
In every step, in every lane,
You are the love that will remain.

In the Depths of the Night

In the depths of the quiet night,
Your love is my guiding light.
When the world is hushed and still,
Your love is my heart's thrill.
In every shadow, in every dream,
You are the light that makes me beam.
Even when darkness clouds the way,
Your love brings a bright new day.
Though the night may stretch so wide,
You are the warmth I feel inside.
In every silence, in every star,
You are my love, no matter how far.
So when the night feels dark and deep,
Know my love for you will keep.
In every moment, in every dream,
You are the love that makes me gleam.

The Gift of Your Love

Your love is a gift I hold so dear,
A treasure that's always near.
In every gesture, in every word,
Your love is the sweetest chord.
Even when the world feels cold,
Your love is the warmth I behold.
A present wrapped in tender grace,
A love that lights up every space.
In every day, in every night,
You are my gift, my heart's delight.
So when you give your love to me,
Know it's the greatest gift I see.
In every moment, in every part,
You are the gift of my heart.
In every touch, in every kiss,
You are my love and eternal bliss.

The Breath of Your Love

Your love is the breath I take each day,
A gentle whisper guiding my way.
In every sigh, in every breeze,
You are the calm that puts me at ease.
With each breath, you fill my soul,
Making me feel utterly whole.
Even when life's winds are strong,
Your love is my soothing song.
In every inhale, in every exhale,
You are the wind in my sail.
So when you breathe, just know this,
Your love is my eternal bliss.
In every breath, in every sigh,
You are the reason my heart flies high.

The Magic of Your Presence

Your presence is a magic spell,
A wondrous tale I know so well.
In every moment that you're near,
My world feels bright and clear.
Your touch, your voice, your gentle way,
Turns every night into day.
Even when the world is bleak and gray,
Your presence lights my way.
In every glance, in every smile,
You make the journey worthwhile.
So when you're here, just know this truth,
Your presence is my eternal youth.
In every moment, in every space,
You are the magic I embrace.

The Calm of Your Love

In the calm of your loving gaze,
I find my heart's eternal blaze.
A soothing peace, a gentle sway,
You turn my night into day.
Even when life seems hard and cold,
Your love is a warmth I behold.
A stillness that brings me rest,
A comfort I know is the best.
In every quiet, in every serene,
You are the calm that I have seen.
So when the world is loud and wild,
Your love is the calm of my inner child.
In every moment, in every calm,
You are the peace that makes me calm.

The Rhythm of Us

Our love has a rhythm, pure and true,
A melody that binds me to you.
In every beat, in every sound,
Our hearts are forever bound.
Even when the tempo changes fast,
Our love's rhythm will always last.
Through every high and every low,
Our love's beat will always show.
In every dance, in every song,
You are the rhythm that makes me strong.
So when you hear our love's sweet tune,
Know it's a song that ends too soon.
In every beat, in every sound,
You are the love that I have found.

The Light in Your Heart

Your heart is a light, so warm and bright,
A beacon that shines through the night.
In every glow, in every beam,
You are the light of my sweetest dream.
Even when shadows start to fall,
Your heart's light is my guiding call.
A radiance that warms my soul,
Making me feel completely whole.
In every shine, in every flare,
You are the light beyond compare.
So when you glow, just know this truth,
Your heart's light is my eternal youth.
In every light, in every gleam,
You are the love of my brightest dream.

The Magic of Your Smile

Your smile is a magic spell so bright,
Turning my world into pure delight.
In every curve, in every beam,
You are the joy within my dream.
Even when the skies are gray,
Your smile brings sunshine to my day.
A charm that brightens every space,
You're the magic in every embrace.
In every laugh, in every grin,
You are the joy that lies within.
So when you smile, just know this true,
Your smile is the love I cherish in you.
In every beam, in every trace,
You are the smile that lights up my place.

The Fire of Our Love

Our love is a fire, burning bright,
A flame that warms me through the night.
In every spark, in every blaze,
You are the light that sets me ablaze.
Even when the winds blow cold,
Our love's fire will never grow old.
A warmth that keeps me near,
A passion that I hold dear.
In every flicker, in every flame,
You are the love that calls my name.
So when the fire starts to rise,
Know my love for you never dies.
In every ember, in every light,
You are my love, my pure delight.

The Magic of Your Voice

Your voice is a melody so sweet,
A song that makes my heart skip a beat.
In every word, in every tone,
You are the love I've always known.
Even when the world feels loud and brash,
Your voice is a gentle, soothing splash.
A serenade that calms my mind,
A love that's tender and kind.
In every whisper, in every call,
You are the magic that I enthrall.
So when you speak, just know this,
Your voice is my eternal bliss.
In every word, in every sound,
You are the love that I have found.

The Comfort of Your Voice

Your voice is a comfort, soft and true,
A melody that brings me to you.
In every tone, in every sound,
A peace that's tenderly profound.
When the world feels harsh and cold,
Your voice is a warmth to behold.
A gentle whisper in the night,
Guiding me with your soothing light.
Even when words are hard to find,
Your voice is a solace to my mind.
So when you speak, just know this true,
Your voice is a gift I cherish in you.
In every sound, in every plea,
You are the calm that comforts me.

The Strength of Your Love

Your love is a strength that never fades,
A power that never evades.
In every touch, in every embrace,
You fill my heart with your grace.
Even when challenges come our way,
Your love is the force that guides my day.
A foundation sturdy and true,
You are the strength I find in you.
In every trial, in every test,
Your love is what makes me feel blessed.
So when the world seems tough and tight,
Know your love is my guiding light.
In every challenge, in every fight,
You are the strength that makes things right.

The Magic of Your Touch

Your touch is a magic that I adore,
A feeling I can't ignore.
In every caress, in every feel,
You are the love that makes me heal.
Even when the world feels tough and wide,
Your touch is my comfort, my guide.
A gentle brush, a tender grace,
You are the calm in every space.
In every moment, in every touch,
You mean more to me than much.
So when you reach out, just know this,
Your touch is my eternal bliss.
In every caress, in every embrace,
You are the love that lights my space.

The Joy of Your Laughter

Your laughter is a joy that I hold dear,
A melody that brings me cheer.
In every chuckle, in every sound,
You are the happiness I've found.
Even when the days are long and gray,
Your laughter brightens every way.
A melody that lifts my soul,
You are the joy that makes me whole.
In every giggle, in every laugh,
You are the love that makes me daft.
So when you laugh, just know this true,
Your laughter is my light in you.
In every sound, in every cheer,
You are the joy that's always near.

The Beauty of Your Soul

Your soul is a beauty that I cherish,
A light that will never perish.
In every gaze, in every sight,
You are the love that feels so right.
Even when the world is dark and cold,
Your soul's beauty is worth more than gold.
A radiance that warms my heart,
You are the masterpiece of art.
In every moment, in every glance,
You are the soul that makes me dance.
So when you shine, just know this true,
Your soul's beauty is my guiding view.
In every light, in every hue,
You are the beauty I see in you.

The Warmth of Your Love

Your love is a warmth that wraps me tight,
A comfort in the darkest night.
In every hug, in every kiss,
You are the warmth that I can't miss.
Even when the cold winds blow,
Your love is a fire that makes me glow.
A heat that keeps me feeling whole,
You are the warmth that touches my soul.
In every touch, in every embrace,
You are the warmth that lights my space.
So when you're near, just know this true,
Your love is the warmth that makes me new.
In every hug, in every kiss,
You are the warmth I truly miss.

The Sweetness of Your Love

Your love is a sweetness I adore,
A flavor I can't ignore.
In every moment, in every taste,
You are the love that I embrace.
Even when the days are long and tough,
Your love is the sweetness I've had enough.
A flavor that makes life so sweet,
You are the love that I will keep.
In every kiss, in every smile,
You are the love that makes life worthwhile.
So when you love, just know this true,
Your sweetness is my joy in you.
In every taste, in every thrill,
You are the love that I feel still.

The Grace of Your Presence

Your presence is a grace that I hold dear,
A light that always brings me near.
In every moment that you are close,
You are the love that I cherish the most.
Even when the world feels harsh and cold,
Your presence is the comfort I behold.
A gentle touch, a soothing way,
You are the grace that brightens my day.
In every space, in every place,
You are the grace I embrace.
So when you're near, just know this true,
Your presence is a gift I cherish in you.
In every moment, in every space,
You are the grace that I embrace.

A Little Note

Though we may be miles apart, my thoughts are with you every single day. Even from a distance, your presence is a constant in my mind, and I cherish you in every moment :)

About the Author

Mrigendra Bharti, born on June 29, 2004, in South Delhi, India, is a multifaceted individual recognized as the owner of Mrigendra Bharti Group InfoTech India Co. Pvt Ltd. Beyond his entrepreneurial endeavors, he is a distinguished music producer, director, and a budding writer.

Embarking on his professional journey at a young age, Mrigendra Bharti's visionary leadership has led to the establishment of several successful ventures, including Croma Music Series Entertainment, Sellbrochure, Fauget Innovative, and more.

What sets Mrigendra apart is his early initiation into the world of business. His foray into the unknown realms of entrepreneurship began during his 10th-grade years, where he delved into the music industry. This initial venture laid the foundation for subsequent achievements, showcasing his dedication and resilience.

Having honed his skills in music, Mrigendra Bharti not only demonstrated significant growth in his craft but also expanded his professional network. His passion extends beyond music, encompassing app and website development, as well as graphic design.

Fueled by his creative aspirations, Mrigendra established the Mrigendra Bharti Group, a company specializing in website and app development. Currently, he collaborates with a dedicated team, collectively working on ambitious projects that promise innovation and excellence.

Mrigendra's journey serves as an inspiration, particularly for today's students, highlighting the potential of youthful determination and the ability to transform innovative ideas into successful businesses. As he continues to make strides in various domains, Mrigendra Bharti remains a dynamic force, contributing vibrancy to the realms of business, music, and technology.

Read more at https://www.imwriter-mrigendra.rf.gd.